חֻקּוֹת הַחַיִּים
A PRACTICAL GUIDE TO
THE LAWS OF KASHRUT

MAGGID

ישיבת
הר עציון
YESHIVAT
HAR ETZION

Pinchas Cohen

חֻקּוֹת הַחַיִּים
A PRACTICAL GUIDE TO THE
LAWS OF KASHRUT

Yeshivat Har Etzion
Alon Shevut
Menachem Av 5770

Maggid Books & Yeshivat Har Etzion

חֻקּוֹת הַחַיִּים
A Practical Guide to the Laws of Kashrut

First Edition 2010

Maggid Books
An Imprint of Koren Publishers Jerusalem Ltd.

POB 8531, New Milford, CT 06776-8531, USA
& POB 2455, London W1A 5WY, England
& POB 4044, Jerusalem 91040, Israel
www.korenpub.com

ISBN 978-1-59264-336-3, *hardcover*

A CIP catalogue record for this title is
available from the British Library.

הרב אהרן ליכטנשטיין
ראש הישיבה

בס"ד
יום שישי י"ב אב תש"ע

This compendium of guidelines and normative Halachic presentation of the major areas of the laws of kashrut as they confront the consumer was written by Rabbi Pinchas Cohen in memory of his father, Rabbi Chaim Cohen זצ"ל, for whom it serves a fitting memento.

The volume attains a twofold purpose. First and foremost, it is oriented to giving the observant Jew, possibly only partially knowledgeable in these areas, practical direction in order to assume proper practice. Concurrently it presents many of the underlying principles so that one's observance is informed by understanding, and not confined to rote performance.

I trust that readers will find the volume succinct and yet informative, a valuable aid in the quest for enhancing a life of religious observance and עבודת השם.

בברכת התורה והמצוה,

Aharon Lichtenstein

Contents

הקדמה.. *xiii*

Introduction... *xv*

Preface..*xvii*

Meat and Milk (בשר בחלב).. 3

   Prohibited Mixtures of Kosher and Non-Kosher Food (תערובות) 4

     Milk cooked in a meat pot on the fire (כלי ראשון).......................... 4

     A utensil that was not used in the last 24 hours (כלי שאינו בן יומו)............. 5

     Milk spoon inserted into meat food...................................... 5

     Milk spoon inserted into pareve food 5

     Cold milk in a meat pot.. 6

     What is halachically considered heat?..................................... 6

     Keli sheni.. 6

     Milk cutlery in meat plates and bowls 7

     Hot meat foods placed on a milk plate.................................... 7

     Cutting cold foods with a knife.. 8

     Cutting hot meat foods with a milk knife 8

     Milk lid placed on a meat pot... 9

     Pickling (כבוש) 9

     Pareve foods that were cooked in meat or milk utensils (נ"ט בר נ"ט) 9

Pareve foods cooked in a milk or meat oven 10

"Sharp" foods (דבר חריף) 10

Separating between Eating Milk and Meat. 12

Eating milk after meat. 12

The time interval between eating meat and milk 13

Eating meat after milk 14

Separation of meat and milk eaten at the table 14

Immersing Utensils (טבילת כלים) 15

Materials that Require Immersion: 15

Immersion of electrical appliances 16

May a guest eat where utensils were not immersed? 17

How to Kasher a Kitchen 19

Cooking utensils and appliances 19

Metal, completely smooth wooden utensils and plastic (pots, cutlery): 19

Glass, pyrex, duralex 20

Ceramics 21

Frying pans. 21

Microwave 21

Sink 21

Dishwasher. 21

Oven. 22

Oven trays. 22

Gas stove 22

Electric stove. 22

Sandwich maker 22

Counter 23

Shabbat plata 23

Using Appliances in a Kosher Kitchen. 25

The stove 25

Oven. 25

Microwave 26

Sink 27

Dishwasher. 27

Insects in Food 29

Introductory principles regarding nullification of insects in a mixture 29

When is there an obligation to check fruits and vegetables before consumption?.... 30

Which fruits and vegetables have to be checked?................................31

    Not infested..31

    Rarely infested 31

    Significant minority are infested (מיעוט המצוי)..........................31

    Infested 31

How does one check?...31

    Apricots...31

    Black Sunflower Seeds..32

    Broccoli 32

    Cabbage 32

    Cauliflower...32

    Celery..32

    Corn on the cob 32

    Dates 32

    Dry beans 33

    Dry figs 33

    Figs 33

    Flour...33

    Lettuce 33

    Nuts 34

    Parsley 34

    Peanuts 34

    Pecan nuts...34

    Rice (and other legumes) 34

    Spinach 34

    Spring onions...35

    Strawberries..35

Gelatin.. 37

Foods of Non-Jews 39

    Milk of Non-Jews (חלב עכו"ם)..................................... 39

        Milk powder.. 40

    Cheese of Non-Jews (גבינת עכו"ם)................................... 41

        Cottage Cheese and Cream Cheese............................... 41

    Bread of Non-Jews (פת עכו"ם)..................................... 42

    Cooking by Non-Jews (בישול עכו"ם)................................. 43

Which foods were included in the prohibition of bishul akum? 43

What level of Jewish participation is required in order to permit the food?..... 43

Wine of Non-Jews (סתם יינם)...44

Glatt Kosher Meat (בשר חלק)......................................47

Kashering Liver...49

Kashrut of Eggs...51

Separation of Challa 53

Separation of Tithes (הפרשת תרומות ומעשרות) 55

Introductory concepts...56

How to separate tithes 57

Nusach of Separation of Tithes...60

Glossary 63

About the Author 67

מאת ראש הישיבה הרב ברוך גיגי שליט"א

נשאו ליבו של ר"מ בית מדרשנו הרב פינחס כהן שליט"א, להעלות על הכתב סיכומי הלכות בענייני כשרות, מפרי עמלו שעמל בהוראת תלמידינו מחו"ל.

קשה להפריז בחשיבות לימוד הלכות הנוגעות למעשה, שהרי ידוע לכל בר בי רב, שלא עם הארץ חסיד ולא בור ירא חטא. ובאופן מיוחד בתחום זה שרבו בו מאוד הפרטים, ויש צורך גדול בפישוט הנושאים ובהסברה מתאימה כדי להנחיל תחום דעת זה לצעירי הצאן.

עם ישראל, ממלכת כהנים וגוי קדוש, נדרש לשמור על קדושתו ולא להתגעל במאכלות אסורים המטמאים את הנפש ואת הגוף, כפי שהדגישה התורה פעמים רבות: 'והתקדשתם והייתם קדושים', 'כי עם קדוש אתה לה' א-להיך'...וכך מסיים הרמב"ם את הלכות מאכלות אסורות: 'וכל הנזהר בדברים אלו מביא קדושה וטהרה יתירה לנפשו, וממרק נפשו לשם הקב"ה שנאמר והתקדשתם והייתם קדושים כי קדוש אני'.

בברכות ק"ש אנו מבקשים: 'ותן בליבנו בינה להבין ולהשכיל לשמוע ללמוד וללמד, לשמור ולעשות ולקיים את כל דברי תלמוד תורתך באהבה'. יש בחיבור זה משום ללמוד ומשום ללמד, ומעל לכול יש בו כדי לתת כלים לעשייה ולקיום של מצוות ה'. ולא ללמד על עצמו יצא, אלא ללמד על הכלל כולו, של חיבור שבין לימוד לעשייה וקיום בכל מרחבי התורה והחיים.

ובכן, אמינא יישר חיליה של הרב פינחס על מעשהו הכפול, הרבצת התורה בע"פ,
והעלאתה על הכתב למען יעמדו ימים רבים. בדרך זו יפוצו המעיינות חוצה גם מעבר
לים לטובת הצעירים הלומדים בכל אתר ואתר.

בהוקרה וידידות אמיצה
ברוך גיגי

Introduction

by the Rosh HaYeshiva HaRav Baruch Gigi

Rav Pinchas Cohen, *shelita*, a Ram in our Yeshiva, has decided to publish a halachic compendium dealing with kashrut-related issues, based on the classes that he gave to the foreign students in our Yeshiva on these matters.

It is difficult to overstate the importance of studying practical Halacha, for everyone knows that "a boor cannot be sin-fearing, and an ignoramus cannot be pious" (*Pirkei Avot* 2:5). This is especially true in this area where there are an exceedingly large number of details and it is urgently necessary to simplify the issues and explain them in an appropriate manner, so that this body of knowledge can be assimilated by younger students.

The Jewish people, a priestly kingdom and holy nation, have been commanded to safeguard their sanctity and not to contaminate themselves with forbidden foods that defile both body and soul, as the Torah emphasizes many times: "You shall sanctify yourselves, and you shall be holy" (*Vayikra* 11:45), "For you are a holy people to the Lord your God" (*Devarim* 14:21). And similarly the Rambam writes in his

Mishneh Torah (*Hilchot Ma'achalot Assurot* 17:32) as follows: "Whoever is careful about these matters brings extra holiness and purity into his soul and refines his soul for the sake of God's name, as it is stated: 'You shall sanctify yourselves, and you shall be holy, for I am holy.'"

In the blessings recited before the *Shema*, we ask: "Inspire us to understand and discern, to perceive, learn and teach, to observe, do and fulfill gladly all the teachings of your Torah." The present book embodies learning and teaching, and above all it provides the tools to fulfill and observe the commandments of God. It exemplifies the combination of theoretical study and practical application that must be found in all areas of the Torah and our lives.

We extend our congratulations to Rav Pinchas for his twofold accomplishments – for the oral dissemination of Torah in his classes and for the publication of his teachings in written form. In this way the wellsprings of his Torah will gush forth and cross oceans, bringing benefit to young students' world over.

With sincerest appreciation and friendship,
Baruch Gigi

Preface

בְּחֻקּוֹת הַחַיִּים הָלַךְ לְבִלְתִּי עֲשׂוֹת עָוֶל חָיוֹ יִחְיֶה לֹא יָמוּת:
(יחזקאל פרק לג)

This booklet חקות החיים on the laws of kashrut is written in the memory of my father HaRav Chaim Cohen זצ"ל, an איש הלכה who imbued his children with a love and respect for תורה.

It is also dedicated to my mother שתבלל"א, may Hashem bless her with long life and good health with the *nachas* of seeing her children and grandchildren grow in תורה ומידות טובות.

This book is being sent to print soon after to the passing of our beloved Rosh Yeshiva HaRav Yehuda Amital, זצ"ל in whose *dalet amot* I had the *zechut* of sitting for close to a decade. May *Hakadosh Baruch Hu* grant us the strength to carry on his legacy to grow in Torah whilst still remaining sensitive to the needs of *klal yisrael*.

I would like to express my הכרת הטוב:

To the Rashei Yeshiva שליט"א and staff of Yeshivat Har Etzion for granting me the opportunity to learn and teach alongside them.

In reference to this book in particular I would like to thank the Rosh Yeshiva HaRav Aharon Lichtenstein שליט"א who reviewed the manuscript and wrote many helpful comments, enhancing the quality of this volume, and to the Rosh Yeshiva Rav Baruch Gigi and Rav Ezra Bick שליט"א for their encouragement and assistance, and to the Rosh Kollel HaRav Shlomo Levi שליט"א for his shiurim on *issur veheter* and for many hours of patiently clarifying Halachic questions in this area.

To Rav Yosef Zvi Rimon for generously sharing his notes on *hilchot kashrut* which were of great assistance in the writing of this volume.

To Rav Yaacov Francus and Rav David Brofsky for generously giving of their time in reviewing this booklet.

To Mrs. Debra Berkowitz, Rav Dov Karoll, Eitan Mirvis, Alex Tsykin, Daniel Fienberg and Robert Cook for copy-editing this manuscript.

To Uriel Cohen for his invaluable assistance in preparing the layout.

"ומתלמידי יותר מכולם", To my dear *talmidim*, for their questions over the years which served as an impetus for the writing of this booklet.

על כולנה to my wife, Ilana, for her endless support and encouragement in all my endeavors.

ברכת ה' עליכם.

יהי רצון מלפניך ה׳ אלהי
שלא יארע דבר תקלה על ידי,
ולא אכשל בדבר הלכה
וישמחו בי חברי,
ולא אומר על טמא טהור
ולא על טהור טמא,
ולא יכשלו חברי בדבר הלכה
ואשמח בהם.

כי ה׳ יתן חכמה מפיו דעת ותבונה:

Meat and Milk
(בשר בחלב)

The prohibition of eating milk and meat together is mentioned three times in the Torah[1]. Our sages tell us that the reason for this repetition is because the Torah wanted to tell us that, in reality, there are three different prohibitions included in this commandment:[2]

1. Cooking: It is forbidden to cook the meat of a kosher, tame animal with the milk of a kosher, tame animal.[3]
2. Eating: According to Torah law, milk and meat that were cooked together may not be eaten. However, the rabbis forbade eating milk and meat together even if they were never cooked together and both are cold.

---

1. *Shemot 29/19, 34/26; Devarim 14/21.*
2. *Chullin 115b, Shulchan Aruch Y.D. 87/1.*
3. In essence, it is permitted to cook chicken or the meat of a kosher, untamed animal with milk, but only if it is clear that the meat is not from a kosher, tame animal and that the meat is not intended for consumption by Jews.

3. Benefit: One may not gain benefit from the meat of a tame animal that was cooked with milk (e.g., by selling to a non-Jew). If they were mixed together in a cold state (e.g., cold meat sandwich with cheese), there is no prohibition to gain benefit.[4]

PROHIBITED MIXTURES OF KOSHER AND NON-KOSHER FOOD (תערובות)

The laws of mixtures can be divided into two major categories:

1. *Yavesh be-yavesh* (a mixture of dry substances): For example a mixture of three separate, indistinguishable pieces of meat, two of which are kosher and one not. In this instance we follow the Torah principle of going after the majority[5] and all three pieces are permitted.[6]

2. *Lach be-lach* (a mixture of wet substances): For example milk falling into the cholent pot. In this instance the *halacha* applies the principle of *ta'am ke'ikar* – the taste is akin to the actual substance.[7] In other words as long as the taste is present, the *issur* (prohibited food) is present. Since tasting this mixture is obviously problematic, the *halacha* only permits its consumption if there are sixty parts of cholent per part of milk.[8]

Milk cooked in a meat pot on the fire (כלי ראשון)

If one cooks milk in a meat pot, it does not suffice to rinse the pot with water. Since the pot has previously absorbed meat taste, it must be *kashered*[9].

---

4. Similarly, there is no prohibition to gain benefit from meat of an untamed animal or chicken cooked with milk.
5. *Shemot* 23/2.
6. See *Shulchan Aruch* Y.D. 109/1 that it is still forbidden to eat all three pieces at once. On a rabbinic level this law only applies to a piece of meat smaller than a piece one would regularly serve a guest (*chaticha ha-re'uya le'hitkabbed*).
7. *Pesachim* 44a.
8. *Chullin* 97a, *Shulchan Aruch* Y.D. 98,1; for the source of the number sixty see *Chullin* 98a.
9. *Shulchan Aruch* Y.D. 93/1.

Moreover, the milk itself is *treif* and must be thrown out (because it absorbed the meat taste in the pot).

A utensil that was not used in the last 24 hours (כלי שאינו בן יומו)

The *halacha* rules that taste particles in a pot turn stale after 24 hours of not being used, therefore the taste particles subsequently emitted from that pot will also be stale (*noten ta'am li'fgam*). Hence, if one cooks meat in a milk pot that has not been used in the last 24 hours (*eino ben-yomo*), the food is still kosher.[10] Nevertheless, the Sages decreed that the pot still needs to be *kashered* in order to prevent mistakes from occurring.[11]

Milk spoon inserted into meat food

If one inserts a milk spoon into a hot meat stew:

1. If the volume of the food is 60 times greater than that of the spoon – the food and the pot are kosher and only the spoon needs to be *kashered*.
2. If the volume of the food is less than 60 times greater than that of the spoon – the food needs to be thrown away and both the spoon and the pot need to be *kashered*.[12]
3. If the spoon was not *ben-yomo* the food is permitted although the spoon requires *hag'ala* – immersion in a pot of boiling water.[13]

Milk spoon inserted into pareve food

If one inserted a milk spoon into *pareve* food being cooked in a meat pot:

According to Sefaradi custom the pot and spoon are kosher. Furthermore, the food may be eaten at a meat or milk meal.[14]

According to Ashkenazi custom, it depends on whether the pot

---

10. *Ibid.*
11. See *Shulchan Aruch* Y.D. 122/2 that the Rabbis were concerned that if people started initially (*le'chatchila*) cooking meat in milk pots that were not used in the last 24 hours – then they might come to using pots that were used in the past 24 hours (*bnei-yoman*).
12. *Shulchan Aruch* Y.D. 94/1.
13. *Shulchan Aruch* Y.D. 94/4.
14. *Shulchan Aruch* Y.D. 95/3.

and the spoon were *bnei-yoman*. If neither were *bnei-yoman*, the pot and spoon are kosher. Furthermore, the food may be eaten at a milk or meat meal.

If either the pot or the spoon was *eino-ben-yomo* and the other utensil was *ben-yomo*, (for example one stirred vegetables on the stove with a milk *eino-ben-yomo* spoon in a meat *ben-yomo* pot) the food may be eaten, but ideally only on a meat plate at a meat meal.[15] It is the custom to *kasher* the spoon in such a case.[16]

If both the pot and spoon were *bnei-yoman*, the utensils need *kashering* and the food is forbidden unless its volume is sixty times the volume of the spoon. If this is the case, it is permissible to eat the food at a meat or milk meal.[17]

Cold milk in a meat pot

If one pours cold milk into a meat pot – it suffices to rinse out the pot with cold water (since the milk was not absorbed into the pot but was only on its surface).

What is halachically considered heat?

According to the Talmud[18] *yad soledet bo* (so hot that it makes one withdraw one's hand) is considered the minimum level of heat required to facilitate absorption of taste by a utensil. It has been determined that *yad soledet bo* is equivalent to at least 45 degrees Celsius (113 Farenheit).[19]

If milk was heated in a meat pot at a lower temperature, the pot does not need *kashering* and it is sufficient to rinse it out thoroughly.

Keli sheni

Keli sheni is the vessel into which food was transferred from the *keli rishon* i.e., the vessel that was in direct contact with the fire. Halachically since a *keli sheni*'s "walls" are not hot it does not cook to the extent of a *keli*

---

15. *Shach Y.D.* 94/18.
16. *Peri Megadim, Mishbetzot Zahav* 94/9.
17. *Rema ibid.* and *Taz* 95/8.
18. *Shabbat* 40b.
19. *Minchat Shlomo* 1/91.

rishon.[20] Nevertheless the mixture of milk and meat in a *keli sheni* is still problematic as will be explained.[21]

Examples of a *keli sheni* are plates, cups and bowls.

Milk cutlery in meat plates and bowls

Ideally one should not insert a milk spoon into a bowl or cup containing a hot (*yad soledet bo*) meat food. If by mistake the spoon was inserted, then *bedi'eved* (post factum) the food is permitted but:

1. Only if disposing of the food will cause a financial loss[22] (for the exact definition of financial loss one should consult a Rabbi).
2. The vessel needs to be *kashered*.

Hot meat foods placed on a milk plate

According to Ashkenazim, if a hot piece of meat (*yad soledet bo*) was placed on a milk plate, since the meat is a solid – *davar gush* – it retains its heat as if it is still inside the *keli rishon*.

Sefaradim do not subscribe to this stringency, and the laws of *keli sheni* apply to the food placed on the plate.

Therefore, for Ashkenazim:

1. The plate needs to be *kashered* in all instances.
2. If the plate was *eino ben-yomo* (not used for hot food in the last 24 hours) the meat is kosher.
3. If the plate was *ben-yomo*: one is required to cut off, with a knife, a thin slice of the meat that came into contact with the plate (*kedei kellipa*).[23]

---

20. *Shabbat* 40b, Tosafot s.v. *"shema minah"*.
21. See further *Shulchan Aruch* Y.D. 105/2.
22. *Taz* Y.D. 105/4.
23. *Shulchan Aruch* Y.D. 105/3. This is based on the principle known as תתאה גבר, that the lower entity impacts upon the upper one.

Cutting cold foods with a knife

A knife which is normally used for cutting meat retains fats which cannot be removed with regular rinsing. Therefore it is forbidden to cut cheese with a meat knife even if they are both cold.[24]

If one cut hard yellow cheese with a meat knife, one is required to rinse off the cheese.

If one cuts soft fruits with a meat knife and wants to eat them with milk, one must scrape off the layer of fruit which came into contact with the knife.[25]

The above applies even if the knife was not used in the last 24 hours.[26]

Rinsing the fruits will not suffice here since it will cause the fats on them to penetrate deeper.

In order to kasher the knife in these cases, where everything was cold, one must rinse it thoroughly with steel wool and liquid soap.[27]

If one cut bread with a clean milk knife, it is permissible to eat the bread with meat.[28]

Ideally every Jewish home should have two sets of knives, for meat and for milk,[29] and also a *pareve* knife designated only for cutting bread and vegetables.

Cutting hot meat foods with a milk knife

If one cuts a hot piece of meat with a milk knife that is *ben-yomo*[30] – there needs to be 60 times more meat than the blade of the knife in order for the meat to be permitted. Nevertheless, one is required to remove a layer of meat with which the knife made contact from both sides which is approximately 2 cm (*kedei netilla*).[31]

---

24. *Shulchan Aruch* Y.D. 89/4.
25. *Shulchan Aruch* Y.D. 96/5.
26. *Noten ta'am li'fgam* does not apply here since the fat is considered to be present on the surface of the knife rather than absorbed in it.
27. This is the present day equivalent to piercing the knife into soil.
28. *Taz* Y.D. 89/7.
29. *Rema* Y.D. 89/4.
30. Used to cut boiling hot milk food in the last 24 hours.
31. *Shulchan Aruch* Y.D. 105/4.

If the meat was cut in a *keli sheni* (e.g., plate), Sefaradim can be lenient.[32]

If the knife was clean and *eino ben-yomo* then the meat is permitted regardless of the ratio between the knife and the meat.[33]

In both of the above cases the knife requires *hag'ala*.

Milk lid placed on a meat pot

If one mistakenly placed a milk *ben-yomo* lid on top of a meat pot that was on the fire, the pot and the lid need to be *kashered*, and the food is *treif* – since vapor that evaporates from the meat comes into contact with the lid and condenses back into the pot.[34]

If the lid was *eino ben-yomo* only the lid needs to be *kashered*.

Pickling (כבוש)

According to Jewish law, pickled food (food immersed in a liquid for 24 hours) has the same status as cooked food (*kavush ki'mevushal*).[35]

Therefore if one placed a milk food together with a meat food in liquid for 24 hours, both foods are forbidden.

Similarly, if one placed cold milk in a meat pot (not on the fire) for 24 hours, the pot needs to be *kashered*. Nevertheless the milk itself is still considered kosher.[36]

Regarding sharp foods (see pg. 31) the pickling process is much more rapid (6–18 minutes). It is therefore recommended that when storing pickled cucumbers or onions etc., one should use a *pareve* utensil.

Pareve foods that were cooked in meat or milk utensils (נ"ט בר נ"ט)

If potatoes were cooked in a clean meat pot and one would like to eat them with milk:

---

32. As noted above Sefaradim are not stringent with regard to a *Davar Gush*.
33. See *Shach* 94/29.
34. *Shulchan Aruch* Y.D. 93/1.
35. *Shulchan Aruch* Y.D. 105/1. It is important to note that the above principle is rabbinic in nature. Therefore in case of doubt one may be lenient.
36. The reason for this is that the food is only considered cooked after 24 hours, at which time the vessel is not *ben-yomo*, so the pot emits a *ta'am lifgam* and the milk is still kosher!

1. According to the Sefaradi custom one may do so.[37]
2. According to the Ashkenazi custom it is forbidden but we are lenient if:
   a. The potatoes are already mixed with milk.
   b. The potatoes were cooked in a meat pot that was not used for meat in the last 24 hours. (*eino ben-yomo*)

Furthermore:
   a. The potatoes can be eaten on a milk plate (but should be transferred onto the plate with a meat spoon).
   b. One can eat milk after eating the potatoes without waiting.
   c. One may use a milk vessel which is not *ben-yomo* to cook *pareve* food to be eaten with meat, if one does not have a vessel which is *pareve*, or meat, which would be suitable[38].

Pareve foods cooked in a milk or meat oven

If a *pareve* dry food (e.g., bread) was cooked in a clean meat oven one is permitted to eat that food with milk. Likewise, if the food was cooked in a milk oven it may be used with meat.[39]

If one wishes to cook a *pareve* food that contains liquid in an oven previously used for meat, in order to eat it with milk, one should first *kasher* the oven (clean thoroughly and turn on the maximum heat for half an hour). If the *pareve* food was cooked without initially *kashering* the oven one may eat it at a milk meal, but may not mixed eat it together with milk foods.

"Sharp" foods (דבר חריף)

"Sharp" foods are defined as any foods whose taste is as strong, or stronger than, a radish. This includes onions, garlic, horseradish, very salty fish (herring), strong spices, cucumbers pickled in a strong brine etc.

There are 3 stringencies we have regarding "sharp" foods:

---

37. *Shulchan Aruch* Y.D. 95/1. According to Rav Ovadia Yosef, Sefaradim may do this *le'chatchila* (see introduction to *Yalkut Yosef, Isssur veHeter* 3).
38. See *Chochmat Adam* 48/2.
39. *Iggerot Moshe* Y.D. 1/40.

1. Even when they are cold they can absorb the taste of a knife when cut by it, i.e., when they are cut with a meat knife they themselves become meaty.[40]

   Note: this stringency only applies if the knife has been used at some stage with boiling hot meat or milk.

2. The lenient principle of *nat bar nat*, mentioned above regarding a case where a *pareve* food was cooked in a milk or meat utensil, with "sharp" foods. Therefore even if the onions were cooked in a clean meat pot they lose their status of being *pareve* and become meaty.[41]

3. When "sharp" foods come into contact with utensils that have not been used in the last 24 hours for meat/milk (*einam bnei yoman*), they are able to extract the taste out of them and the taste is not considered *ta'am lifgam*.[42]

   Note: Sefaradim can be lenient regarding law 3, in a case of great financial loss.[43]

According to Ashkenazim all stringencies apply.

Therefore:

If one cuts onions with a meat knife, they may not be eaten with milk. However, if the onion was sixty times larger than the amount of the knife which penetrated it, the onion may be eaten after removing two centimeters from each side that came into contact with the knife.

If one cuts onions with a meat knife (that had been used in the past to cut boiling meat) and they are subsequently fried, by themselves,[44] in a milk pan, – the onions are *treif* and the pan needs to be *kashered*. Nevertheless if the onions were prepared in a soup and not fried, the onions remain *pareve*.

One should be careful when serving horseradish (*chrein*) not to use a meat spoon since the spoon can make the *chrein* meaty through pickling.[45]

---

40. *Chullin* 111b, *Shulchan Aruch* Y.D. 96/1.
41. *Rema* Y.D. 95/2.
42. *Avoda Zara* 39a, *Shulchan Aruch* Y.D. 103/6.
43. *Kaf HaChaim* Y.D. 96/10.
44. If the onions were fried together with other non-sharp food *bitul* may occur.
45. Pickling in "sharp" food occurs very rapidly. Opinions vary from 6 to 18 minutes.

If one fries onions, by themselves, in a meat pan and stirs with a milk spoon:

1. If the pot and the spoon are *ben-yomo*, they both need to be *kashered* and the onions are forbidden.
2. If the pot and the spoon are *einam-bnei-yoman* – everything needs *kashering* and the onions are forbidden.
3. When the onions are fried, they take on the status of meat and are no longer classified as "sharp". Hence, if the milk spoon is inserted when the onions were *already fried*:
   a. If the spoon was *ben-yomo* the spoon and the pot need kashering and the onions are forbidden.
   b. If the spoon was *eino-ben-yomo*, the onions and the pot are kosher[46] and only the spoon needs *kashering*.

If one ate an onion cut with a meat knife, one does not have to wait afterwards in order to eat milk.[47]

Note: In order to avoid all of the above problems one should always cut vegetables with a *pareve* knife on a *pareve* board!

SEPARATING BETWEEN EATING MILK AND MEAT
Eating milk after meat
Beyond the Torah prohibition to eat meat (or chicken) and milk that were cooked together, the sages decreed that one may not eat milk immediately after eating meat without an intermission from one meal time to the next.[48]

Two reasons are given for this decree:

---

46. Since the onions now have the status of meat and not "sharp" foods, we do not apply stringency (3) mentioned above.
47. *Chidushei R' Akiva Eiger on Shach* Y.D. 89/19. However, there are opinions that if one eats meat, one should wait 6 hours before eating an onion cut with a milk knife.
48. *Chullin* 105a.

1. After eating meat, some of it remains in one's teeth for six hours and if one eats milk in that time, one is eating meat with milk.[49]
2. Until six hours the meat is not fully digested and one still has the taste of meat in one's mouth.[50]

Halachically both reasons are accepted as valid.[51] Therefore:

If one only chewed on meat but did not swallow, he still has to wait before eating milk (according to reason 1).

If one tasted meat without chewing or swallowing he does not have to wait. However he is required to eat something *pareve* that does not stick to the mouth[52] (*kinu'ach*) and to rinse out his mouth (*hadacha*) before eating milk products.

If the interval has passed and one still has meat between his teeth, the meat has to be removed before eating milk (according to reason 2, since the digestion begins only after swallowing). In this case *kinu'ach* and *hadacha* also have to be performed.

One is required to wait even after eating *pareve* foods that were cooked in the same pot with meat. However, if they were cooked in a clean meat pot there is no obligation to wait.

One who swallows a tablet which contains meat does not have to wait before eating milk but it should not be swallowed together with milk.

The time interval between eating meat and milk

The time interval is counted from the cessation of eating meat and not from the end of the meal.

There are different customs among Jews regarding the time period of this interval: Sefaradim (and many Ashkenazim) generally wait six hours (the time between two meals on an average day).[53] Many

---

49. *Rambam Ma'achalot Assurot* 9/28.
50. *Tur Y.D.* 89.
51. *Shulchan Aruch Y.D.* 89/1.
52. For example a biscuit is recommended whilst dates are not.
53. *Shulchan Aruch Y.D.* 89/1.

Ashkenazim have a custom to wait three hours.[54] The custom of Dutch Jews is to wait one hour.

Children or sick people should ideally wait for one hour.[55]

Eating meat after milk

After eating milk products one does not have to wait in order to eat meat. Nevertheless *hadacha* and *kinu'ach*[56] are required. One is also required to clean one's hands before eating meat after eating cheese.[57]

If one wants to eat chicken after eating milk products one is only required to check that his hands are clean; *hadacha* and *kinu'ach* are not required.[58]

There are those who have the custom to wait after eating hard cheese,[59] for the same amount of time that they would wait after eating meat, in order to eat milk.

Separation of meat and milk eaten at the table

It is forbidden to eat meat at a table which has milk placed on it and vice versa.[60]

Similarly it is forbidden to eat meat at a table where someone else is eating a milk meal out of concern that one will come to partake of the other's meal.

In order for this to be permitted one is required to change something at the table, e.g., placing an object on the table that is not usually found there as a separation, or eating on different place mats.

A table cloth that was used for a milk meal may not be eaten on directly during a meat meal and vice versa.[61]

---

54. See Rabeinu Yerucham Issur Ve'heter 39, *Peri Chadash* 89/6 and *Darchei Teshuva* 89/1/6 in the name of the *Mizmor leDavid*.

55. HaRav Shlomo Levi, *shlita*; see also *Yabia Omer* Y.D. 1/4.

56. There are *posekim* who maintain that if one only drank milk and did not eat cheese one does not need *kinu'ach* and *hadacha* is sufficient.

57. *Shulchan Aruch* Y.D. 89/2.

58. Since the prohibition to eat chicken with milk is only of rabbinic origin.

59. Blue Cheese (*Taz* Y.D. 89/4) or cheese that has undergone an ageing process of six months (*Shach* Y.D. 89/15).

60. *Shulchan Aruch* Y.D. 88/1.

61. *Shulchan Aruch* Y.D. 89/4 with *Pitchei Teshuva ad loc.*

Immersing Utensils
(טבילת כלים)

One who purchases or receives eating or drinking utensils from a non-Jew is required to immerse them in a kosher *mikveh* in order to sanctify them for Jewish use.[1]

Furthermore utensils that are used in the preparation of the meal require immersion (e.g., pots and pans). However if the food still requires further preparation after the utensil has been used (e.g., a potato peeler) immersion should be performed without a *beracha*.[2]

Utensils used for storage only, which come into direct contact with the food (e.g., a coffee jar), require immersion without a *beracha*.[3]

MATERIALS THAT REQUIRE IMMERSION:

1. Metal utensils require immersion according to Torah law.

---

1. *Bamidbar* 31, *Avodah Zarah* 75b.
2. See *Shulchan Aruch* Y.D. 120/5.
3. See *Darchei Teshuva* Y.D. 120/6.

2. Glassware (including Pyrex and Duralex) requires immersion according to rabbinic law.
3. Clay and wood vessels are exempt from immersion.
4. Porcelain[4] and plastic[5] dishes do not require immersion, yet there are those who are stringent and immerse but without a *beracha.*[6]

If one is immersing a non-kosher dish, it should first be *kashered.*[7]

If one bought a vessel from a company owned by a Jew, even if its workers are non-Jewish, immersion is not required.[8]

At the time of immersion the utensil should be as clean as possible and one should remove any stickers from its surface.[9]

There should be no separation preventing the water of the *mikveh* from making contact with every part of the utensil (including the handles) and therefore one should not hold the utensil too tightly or should wet one's hands before immersing.[10]

Immersion of electrical appliances

There are numerous opinions regarding ways to halachically avoid the immersion of electrical appliances and we will list them in order of preference:

1. Giving the appliance to a Jewish technician who can dismantle a vital component of the appliance and reassemble it (putting on the plug does not suffice).[11]

---

4. *Minchat Yitzchak* 4/114.
5. *Yechaveh Da'at* 3/60.
6. *Kitzur Shulchan Aruch* 37/3 regarding porcelain and *Kinyan Torah* 2/84 regarding plastic.
7. *Shulchan Aruch* Y.D. 121/2.
8. *Iggerot Moshe* O.C. 3/4.
9. *Shulchan Aruch* Y.D. 120/13.
10. *Shulchan Aruch* Y.D. 120/2.
11. Rav S.Z. Auerbach זצ"ל based on the *Chochmat Adam* 73/13. Through this the utensil is considered to be made by a Jew and therefore does not require immersion.

2. One can give the appliance to a non-Jew and consequently borrow it from him.[12]

3. Some *posekim* maintain that the mere connection of the appliance's plug to the socket exempts it from immersion.[13]

4. If practical, there are those who are of the opinion that only the part of the appliance that comes in direct contact with the food requires immersion.[14]

5. There are opinions that electrical appliances do not require immersion at all.[15]

Note: there are pious people who immerse their electrical appliances like all other utensils (one should be careful to let them dry **properly** before usage!).

May a guest eat where utensils were not immersed?

In this matter there is room to be lenient, although if there is a possibility of eating from porcelain, plastic or disposable dishes it is preferable.[16]

Eating in a hotel or restaurant whose utensils were not immersed is permitted.[17]

12. *Minchat Yitzchak* 5/126/2 based on *Shulchan Aruch* O.C. 323/7.
13. *Chelkat Ya'acov* Y.D. 41. The logic behind this being that according to *halacha* only moveable utensils require immersion and therefore when the appliance is connected to the wall it is no longer considered moveable!
14. *Iggerot Moshe* Y.D. 1/57.
15. HaRav Yehuda Amital זצ"ל. *Iggerot Moshe* Y.D. 3/24 is lenient regarding a toaster since the food inserted is already baked.
16. *Beit Avi* 116, *Da'at Kohen* 227.
17. *Yechaveh Da'at* 4/44.

How to Kasher a Kitchen

Afundamental principle which is the basis of the entire kashering process is *"ke'vol'o-kach poleto"* – that taste (or prohibited matter) is removed from a utensil in the same way that the utensil absorbed it.[1]

For example: a utensil which became non-kosher through direct contact with fire (an oven tray) would have to be burned at high temperature, while a utensil which became non-kosher through boiling (regular pot on the stove) would have to be *kashered* in boiling water.

COOKING UTENSILS AND APPLIANCES

Metal, completely smooth wooden utensils and plastic[2] (pots, cutlery):

1. Clean the utensils that you want to kasher.[3]

---

1. See *Rashi, Bamidbar* 31/23, *Pesachim* 74a.
2. According to the *Minchat Yitzchak* 3/67 and the *Chelkat Ya'acov* Y.D. 45, these rules apply to plastic as well. The *Iggerot Moshe* E.H. 4/7 agrees with their ruling regarding *kashering* generally but not for Pesach, regarding which he rules (O.C. 2/92) that plastic cannot be *kashered*.
3. *Shulchan Aruch* O.C. 451/3.

2. Leave the utensils unused for 24 hours[4] (unless the volume of water in the pot will be 60 times greater than that of the utensils) or add soapy water to the pot in which the utensils will be *kashered*.[5]

3. Take a big clean pot for the utensils to be *kashered* in, fill it with water and bring it to boiling point. It must remain at this temperature or higher throughout the entire kashering process.

4. Place the utensil completely in the pot of boiling water (*hag'ala*).

   a. One should not place too many utensils in the pot at the same time.

   b. If a utensil is too big to be placed fully in the pot at once, one may place the utensil in the pot part by part, provided that by the end all parts of the utensil have been fully immersed.[6]

3. Place the utensil in cold water.[7]

Glass, pyrex, duralex

Meat and milk

Sefaradim: Can be rinsed thoroughly in cold water.[8]

Ashkenazim: During the year – if the utensil came into direct contact with fire one can do *hag'ala*[9] after not using the utensil for 24 hours.

Glass plates cups and bowls etc. may be *kashered* by thorough rinsing in cold water. [10]

Pesach

If a *chametz* utensil came into direct contact with fire it is better to replace it.

Regarding glass plates, cups and bowls etc., when necessary,

---

4. *Shulchan Aruch* Y.D. 121/2.
5. *Shulchan Aruch* Y.D. 95/4.
6. *Shulchan Aruch* O.C. 451/3.
7. *Shulchan Aruch* O.C. 452/7. This is preferable but not critical.
8. *Shulchan Aruch* O.C. 451/26.
9. However one should be careful **not** to put the utensil into cold water after *hag'ala* since it might shatter.
10. See *Peri Megadim* O.C. 451/31

one can do *hag'ala* or soak them in water for 3 days, changing the water every 24 hours.[11]

Ceramics

If generally not used in direct contact with fire, e.g., plates, bowls and cutlery: If there is no other alternative – one can be lenient and do *hag'ala* three times after waiting for 24 hours.[12]

Frying pans

1. If used with oil:

    Ideally one should perform *libbun kal* i.e., holding the pan up to a fire for the amount of time that the pan will warm up to the extent that the side which is not in contact with fire will burn a piece of straw or a matchstick.

    If *libbun kal* is not possible one may do *hag'ala* after cleaning and not using the utensil for 24 hours.[13]

2. If used without oil – the frying pan should be replaced.

Microwave[14]

1. Clean thoroughly.
2. Leave unused for 24 hours.
3. Cook a cup of soapy water for a few minutes.[15]

Sink

1. Clean thoroughly.
2. Pour hot water from a boiling kettle all over the sink.

Dishwasher

1. Clean thoroughly.

11. *Mishna Berura* 451/156.
12. Rav Mordechai Eliyahu זצ"ל based on the opinion the *Ba'al Ha'Itur* brought down in the *Tur* Y.D. 121. See also *Iggerot Moshe* Y.D. 2/46.
13. *Rema* 451/4.
14. To *kasher* a microwave for Pesach one should, in addition to the above, cover all foods inserted.
15. Rav Moshe Feinstein quoted in *Halachos of Pesach* by Rav Shimon Eider.

2. Leave unused for 24 hours.
3. Do *hag'ala* on strainer and dish racks or at least pour boiling water over them and place them in the dishwasher at the time of *kashering*.
4. Run a full cycle on maximum heat.

Oven

1. Clean thoroughly with oven cleaner.
2. Leave unused for 24 hours.
3. Turn oven on maximum heat for an hour.

Oven trays

1. If the food is placed on them directly, they should be blow-torched or replaced.
2. If the food is not placed on them directly, one should clean them, wait 24 hours and place them in the oven at the time of kashering.

Gas stove

1. Surface – clean thoroughly.
2. Burners – turn on for half an hour.
3. Grids – try to replace or at least to do *libbun kal*.

Electric stove

1. Clean thoroughly.
2. Do not use for 24 hours.
3. Operate for half an hour.

Sandwich maker[16]

1. Clean thoroughly with oven cleaner.
2. Leave unused for 24 hours.
3. Turn it on for half an hour with nothing inside.

---

16. One should only *kasher* a sandwich maker if there is a significant need and only for during the year, not for *Pesach*.

Counter

1. Clean thoroughly.
2. Pour boiling hot water over it.
3. For Pesach it would be sufficient to adequately clean and cover the counter (e.g., with thick tinfoil, cardboard etc.).

Shabbat plata

1. Clean thoroughly.
2. Operate for an hour.
3. Cover with tin foil.

Using Appliances in a Kosher Kitchen

The stove

One is allowed to use the same stove for meat and milk pots since, even if some of the contents spill over, the fire will consume them immediately.[1]

If a drop of milk splashes onto a meat pot while it is on the fire – in many cases the pot will need to be *kashered*. It is therefore advisable to consult a Rabbi if this occurs.[2]

The stovetop and its grids are generally *treif*. Therefore if food falls onto them it is generally recommended to dispose of it. Similarly, one should not place cutlery in this area.

Oven

According to *halacha* the steam emanating from the food (זיעה) is considered like the food itself.[3] Therefore when cooking a meat dish in the oven, the vapor will be absorbed by the oven walls. Consequently, when one later cooks milk, the meat vapor will descend into the milk dish thereby making it *treif*.

---

1. *Mishna Berura* 451/34.
2. See *Shulchan Aruch* Y.D. 92/5.
3. *Shut HaRosh* 20/26 based on *Mishna, Machshirin* 2/2.

How should an oven be used in a Jewish home for meat and milk? We will list the options in order of preference:

1. Ideally one should purchase an oven with two compartments to be used separately for meat and milk.

2. If the oven has only one compartment, one should always cover the food one is baking. If this is difficult, one can use the oven to prepare meat, for example, foods uncovered, and when one chooses to prepare a milk dish, one should clean the grid and place the food in a covered milk tray.

3. Between baking meat and milk dishes, one should wait 24 hours and turn on the oven to maximum heat for half an hour. One can then cook milk in the oven even without a cover.

4. In a home where the previous options will not be accepted, one can turn on the oven between meat and milk for half an hour without the 24 hour wait.[4]

5. Regarding dry baked products, for example pastries which consist of cheese or meat, one is not required to wait 24 hours or turn on the oven for half an hour since they do not produce vapor.[5]

6. In a home in which none of the previous solutions will be adhered to (e.g., a child in a home with non-observant parents), one may cook meat in an oven previously used for milk, as long as the oven was cleaned between the cooking of meat and milk.[6]

Microwave

A microwave can be used for meat and milk provided that either the meat or the milk dishes are always covered (with a plastic bag or the like).

If one mistakenly heated a piece of meat in a microwave on a milk plate, the plate must be *kashered*[7] and the piece of meat is *treif*.

---

4. See *Yabia Omer* Y.D. 5/7.
5. *Iggerot Moshe* Y.D. 1/40,59
6. Rav Hershel Schachter related to me that based on the *Darchei Teshuva* 92/8/165 one can rely on this opinion even *lechatchila*.
7. This applies to a glass plate; if the plate was ceramic or porcelain one should consult a Rabbi.

Sink

Since the dishes in the sink usually have fatty residue and are dirty, one should not wash milk and meat dishes simultaneously in the same sink.

Can one wash meat and milk dishes in the same sink one after another?

Ideally not, but clearly if it was done then ex-post-facto the dishes are still kosher.[8]

In a house that has only one sink, meat and milk dishes can be washed inside it but not simultaneously.[9]

Dishwasher

One should not wash meat and milk dishes simultaneously in a dishwasher since this could involve the cooking of meat and milk residues which will consequently make the utensils *treif*. If this occurred then ex-post-facto there is room to be lenient since the liquid soap will give a *ta'am li'fgam*.[10]

Can one wash dishes one after the other in a dishwasher?

Ideally it is recommended to use the dishwasher for either meat or milk only. If this is not possible it is permitted to use the machine for both, if one designates different racks for meat and milk utensils.[11]

With regards to the latest models of dishwashers, where the washing detergent is activated at a later stage in the washing cycle, the successive washing of milk and meat dishes is more problematic. It is therefore recommended to insert some liquid soap into the main compartment in order to facilitate a *ta'am lifgam* at an earlier stage and to wash out the strainers between cycles of meat and milk.

---

8. See *Shulchan Aruch* Y.D. 95/3 and *Iggerot Moshe* Y.D. 1/42.
9. HaRav Amital, זצ"ל, *Yalkut Yosef, Isssur veHeter* 3/89/80. If possible the water should not be over 45 degrees (113F) or separate grids should be used for meat and milk dishes.
10. See *Kitzur Shulchan Aruch, Hilchot Basar beChalav* (Rav Pfueffer זצ"ל) Section 2 page 138.
11. *Iggerot Moshe* O.C. 1/104, Y.D. 2/28,29. The reason for this leniency is due to the fact that there is *bitul beshishim* regarding food substances that might be absorbed in the walls, and that the soap gives a *ta'am lifgam*.

Insects in Food

I n many places, the Torah prohibits the eating of insects. This is a very grave sin involving the transgression of 4–6 negative commandments.[1] As a result, one has to check fruits and vegetables for insects even if they are found in a very small minority of cases.

INTRODUCTORY PRINCIPLES REGARDING NULLIFICATION OF INSECTS IN A MIXTURE

1. Generally when forbidden food (*issur*) falls into permitted food (*heter*) that has sixty times its volume, nullification (*bitul*) occurs. However, the Rabbis decreed that regarding intact living creatures (*birya*) nullification does not occur. In this case the transgression is Rabbinic.[2]

2. If the insect was mixed (mistakenly) with food and is no longer intact then nullification occurs as usual.[3]

---

1. See *Makkot* 16b
2. *Shulchan Aruch* Y.D. 100/1.
3. *Ibid.*

WHEN IS THERE AN OBLIGATION TO CHECK FRUITS
AND VEGETABLES BEFORE CONSUMPTION?

Each type of fruit and vegetable falls under one of these categories, each with its own level of stringency:

1. An insignificant minority is infested (*mi'ut she'eino matzuy*). Insects are found very rarely on these fruits and vegetables. Consequently they do not require checking.
2. A significant minority (usually defined as at least 10%)[4] is infested (*mi'ut hamatzuy*). Consequently, these fruits and vegetables do require checking on a rabbinic level. [5] However if these food types have already been blended in a mixture or baked, the final dish may be eaten. For example, if a cake was baked and the flour used was not checked, the cake is permitted.[6]
3. Fruits which are almost always infested (*muchzak menuga*). These always have to be checked and are forbidden to be eaten if not previously checked. Therefore if one is a guest at a house where there is a doubt whether the lettuce was checked, one may not eat the salad.[7] Even if the fruits or vegetables have already been cooked or baked the mixture is still forbidden.[8] There is one situation, however in which one may be lenient. This is when

---

4. *Mishkenot Ya'akov* 17. This opinion was also accepted by Rav Shomo Zalman Aurbach z.t.l. (*Bedikat Hamazon baHalacha* pg. 81). For other opinions see *Shut HaRivash* 191 and *Shevet Halevi* 4/81.
5. *Shach* Y.D. 39/8, *Siftei Da'at* 84/28.
6. *Shulchan Aruch* Y.D. 84/9 and *Taz* ibid 17. Firstly, there is a doubt whether there are insects in the mixture creating a *safek deRabbanan*. Secondly, even if there are insects present, the insects are probably dismembered, creating a second *safek deRabbanan*.
7. Although the *issur* (insect) seems to be mixed together with the *heter* (salad leaves), according to *Halacha* if the *issur* is recognizable it is not considered to be a *ta'arovet* (a 'halachic mixture'). There is a debate among the *posekim* whether a mixture in which the *issur* may only be recognized with great effort is considered a *ta'arovet*. According to the opinions that hold that the salad is not a *ta'arovet*, its eating will constitute an *issur de'oraita* (*Chochmat Adam* 51/1). However, according to those who rule the salad is a *ta'arovet*, its eating represents only a rabbinic prohibition (*Aruch haShulchan* Y.D. 100/7).
8. *Shach* Y.D. 84/29.

these fruits have been **inadvertently** ground or crushed before checking. Even though the fruits are almost always infested with insects if there is sixty times more fruit than insect, the food may be eaten since once an insect is dismembered nullification in sixty can occur.[9]

WHICH FRUITS AND VEGETABLES HAVE TO BE CHECKED?

Note: The following is only applicable to Israeli produce and if one is overseas one should consult an halachic authority from that country.

Not infested
Avocado, watermelon, pineapple, okra, white sunflower seeds, rice cakes, white raisins, kohlrabi, coconut, cornflakes, cinnamon, coffee, sugar, tinned corn, potato flour, potatoes.

Rarely infested
Soup mix, mushrooms, and bread crumbs.

Significant minority are infested (מיעוט המצוי)
Peanuts, barley, granola, chickpeas, wheat, spelt, apricot, bran, red lentils, black raisins, rice, flour, matza meal, loquat, beans, almonds, dates.

Infested
Asparagus, artichoke, green onions, broccoli, guava, black sunflower seeds, skin of carp fish, lettuce, carobs, cabbage, cauliflower, leeks, celery, brown lentils, parsley, emery, coriander, mint, sweet basil, figs (especially dry figs), strawberries, corn, spinach.

HOW DOES ONE CHECK?

Apricots
Black spots on the outside are not a sign of infestation.
Fresh apricots: one should take out the pit and check.
Dry apricots: halve, wash in warm water and check.

---

9. See *Shulchan Aruch* Y.D. 101/6.

Black Sunflower Seeds

In every handful take out the blemished seeds; check occasionally. If one finds three that are infested they should all be checked.

Broccoli

Similar to cauliflower (see below). Dispose of the upper leaves. The stalks should be soaked in soap water and washed thoroughly. Ideally one should try to buy חסלט.

Cabbage

Throw away the top leaves, separate the rest of the leaves, soak for three minutes in dishwashing liquid, rinse each leaf under the tap.

Cauliflower

Very difficult to check. Therefore, one should ideally buy חסלט (vegetables grown in insect-free green-houses).

If not, the flower should be thrown away. The stalk and branches should be soaked in soapy water and rinsed. It is recommended to cut some of the stalks in half and check.

Celery

Separate the stalks and leaves.
Stalks: scrub well from both sides.
Leaves: remove stained leaves. The rest of the leaves should be soaked in soap water and then rinsed.

Corn on the cob

Check externally. Separate three kernels of each cob and check well. If infested, it can only be eaten after checking each and every kernel individually.

Dates

Open them and extract the pit, check under light for any insects.

Dry beans

Boil them in water twice as much as their volume, turn off the flame and leave them covered for two hours. Consequently the beans will become transparent. Check the beans by passing them from hand to hand. If a certain area has a dark stain, it very likely to be infested.

If one is pressed for time (e.g., *erev Shabbat*) and one has a large quantity, it would be sufficient to thoroughly check each individual bean.

Dry figs
Very difficult to check. One should rinse, check for unnatural holes, halve and check under strong light – if any area is black it usually means that it is infested.

Figs
Cut open, fold outwards and check. Place them in water with the opening facing downwards in a transparent glass of water. If there are insects they will float to the top.

Flour
One should sift the flour in a fine sieve (at least 40×40 holes per square inch). It is sufficient to check one cup per kilogram packet.[10] After sifting, if one places the flour in the freezer, it does not have to be checked again. Flour that was acquired within three days of being ground does not have to be checked.

Lettuce
There are two ways to check lettuce:

1. The conventional way is to wash the leaves and then check each leaf individually using strong light.
2. Today experts have reached a conclusion that there is an easier and more effective way:
   a. Separating the leaves
   b. Soaking the leaves in water with some dishwashing liquid for 3 minutes
   c. Wiping off each leaf with a cloth from both sides
4. *"Gush Katif"* vegetables do not need to be checked. Occasionally

---

10. See *Aruch haShulchan* 84/65.

insects may be found on the surface, so one should rinse them before eating and follow any other instructions on the packet.

Nuts

If there are strands, then the nuts are infested and should be thrown away. The same rule applies if there are many crumbs.

Parsley

If it is added for taste only, then it is preferable to cook it while wrapped in a packet. If it is meant for consumption one should remove the stained leaves, soak them in soapy water, take a small bunch of leaves and scrub with a sponge from both sides, and rinse and grind them in a food processor.

Dry parsley is generally ok, yet one should check that no worms have penetrated the parsley after its dehydration.

Peanuts

Check externally.

Pecan nuts

Do not need to be checked.

Rice (and other legumes)

The problem with rice is not the occurrence of insects in the grains themselves but insects found between the grains. When buying rice one should check that there is no grind found underneath the rice. So too, one should check between the grains for small black, brown or white insects.

Spinach

Should be cleaned like cabbage.

Spring onions

White root is clean.

In order to check the leaves, take one onion from the batch and cut its leaves lengthwise.

If three insects are found, all of the leaves of the remaining onions need to be checked.

If less than three insects are found, or if the onion is clean, only one leaf of each remaining onion needs to be checked. If an insect is found, all the leaves of that onion need to be checked.

Strawberries
Cut the green leaf with a millimeter of the fruit. Soak in soap water for three minutes, wash under the tap.

Gelatin

Gelatin is an inedible solid substance which is commonly used as a gelling agent in food. It is prepared by the partial hydrolysis of collagen, a substance found in the bones, connective tissues, organs and some intestines of cattle, pigs and horses. Almost all gelatin used in the food industry today is derived from non-kosher animals or animals that have not been slaughtered in accordance with *halacha*.

This process gives rise to a question that has been the source of much halachic debate: if non-kosher food becomes inedible, is it no longer classified as food, thereby losing its non-kosher status?

Practically speaking one should try avoiding eating gelatin.[1] Nevertheless if one is in need there is room to be lenient.[2]

1. *Iggerot Moshe* Y.D. 2/23.
2. *Achi'ezer* 3/33/5.

Foods of Non-Jews

There are many situations where, even though food produced by non-Jews is technically completely kosher, the sages decreed that it is forbidden to eat. The reason for this is generally either that the sages were worried that the gentile added something non-kosher to the food or that they wanted to prevent us from overly friendly interaction with non-Jews which may lead to intermarriage.

This prohibition manifests itself in five areas:

1. חלב עכו"ם (milk of non-Jews)
2. גבינת עכו"ם (cheese of non-Jews)
3. פת עכו"ם (bread of non-Jews)
4. בישול עכו"ם (cooking of non-Jews)
5. יין נסך וסתם יינם (wine of non-Jews)

MILK OF NON-JEWS (חלב עכו"ם)

The rabbis were concerned about a situation where a gentile might mix the milk from a kosher animal with that of a non-kosher animal. Therefore they issued a decree that any milking that is not supervised by a Jew

39

renders the milk not kosher.[1] According to the strict interpretation of this law, most milk today in the Diaspora would be prohibited.

Nevertheless, there are halachic authorities who hold that when this suspicion does not exist, the decree is no longer applicable.[2] For example, if a non-Jew has no non-kosher animals in his herd. Similarly, if there are no non-kosher animals in the entire region. Furthermore, there is also room to be lenient if non-kosher milk is only commercially available at a much greater expense, making tampering with kosher milk commercially unviable.[3]

A second consideration for leniency is based on the Talmud's definition of supervision[4]. According to the Talmud, even if the Jew is not constantly observing the milking process, but the non-Jew fears that at any given time there is a strong chance that the Jew may appear unexpectedly, then the milk still retains its status as having being supervised by a Jew, and remains kosher.

Rabbi Moshe Feinstein applied this logic to government supervised milk. He suggested that since the milk companies are under governmental supervision, and the owners will be fined heavily if they are caught tampering with the milk, the milk remains permissible to drink.

It is important to note that Rabbi Feinstein himself writes that he did not drink government supervised milk.[5]

Today the O.U. in America is lenient on this issue as opposed to *mehadrin hechsherim* in Israel which do not use *chalav akum*.[6]

Milk powder

Even among those who are stringent regarding *chalav akum*, there are those who permit using milk powder of non-Jews since the decree was

---

1. *Avodah Zarah* 35b.
2. *Shut Radvaz* 4/75.
3. *Peri Chadash* Y.D. 115/6.
4. *Avodah Zarah* 39b.
5. *Iggerot Moshe* Y.D. 1/47.
6. The Rabanut *hechsher* in Israel is only lenient regarding non-Jewish milk powder but are stringent regarding the milk itself. (*Bi'ntiv haChalav* pg. 40 – Rav Ze'ev Weitman)

only passed on liquid milk.[7] Similarly one may be lenient and allow young children to eat products with non-Jewish milk-powder.[8]

CHEESE OF NON-JEWS (גבינת עכו"ם)

Even though milk of non-kosher animals cannot curdle into cheese, the sages forbade cheese made by non-Jews for fear that the gentile might have curdled it in the stomach of a forbidden animal, thereby making the resultant cheese not kosher.[9] Today cheese is made by adding rennet which is an enzyme produced in the stomach of non-kosher animals, and is often used in the production of cheese.

The law regarding cheese made by non-Jews is more stringent than with milk. The reason is that we are concerned about opinions that subscribe to the view that the sages forbade cheese made by non-Jews in order to place a social boundary between Jews and non-Jews, aside from the concern for *kashrut*.[10]

For cheese made by non-Jews to be kosher, some argue that it does not suffice for a Jew to merely supervise the manufacturing process. Rather, a Jew is required to *participate* in making it.[11]

Cottage Cheese and Cream Cheese

The halachic status of cottage and cream cheese during the ageing process is a matter of dispute between the *posekim*. Although it is made without adding rennet, it is made by fermenting the cheese, naturally or by adding acids, resulting in the coagulation of the milk.

Some *posekim* classify these soft cheeses as milk and by extension, Rav Feinstein's aforementioned leniency may be applied.[12] However,

7. *Har Tzvi* Y.D. 103.
8. *Yalkut Yosef Issur veHeter* 2/81/14.
9. *Avodah Zarah* 29b. See also *Avodah Zarah* 35b where more reasons are listed, although the above reason is the only one recorded by the *Rambam, Ma'achalot Assurot* 3/13 and *Shulchan Aruch* Y.D. 115/2.
10. *Maggid Mishneh* ibid.
11. *Shach* Y.D. 115/20 and *Gra* ibid. 14. Even though the *Rema* Y.D. 115/2 is lenient in this regard, most *kashrut* organizations today follow the stringency of the *Shach*. (Rav Weitman *Bi'ntiv haChalav* pg. 53)
12. *Peri Chadash* 115/21. Rav Moshe Feinstein himself writes that although these cheeses

others feel that these soft cheeses fall under the same category as hard cheeses and are therefore included in the stricter prohibition of *gevinat akum.*[13]

BREAD OF NON-JEWS (פת עכו״ם)

The sages banned the bread of non-Jews in order to prevent excessive socializing with them, which may lead to intermarriage (which could in turn lead to idol worship).[14]

Bread is considered "Jewish" if a Jew:

1.   Turned on the oven; or
2.   Threw a match into the oven; or
3.   Placed the bread in the oven.[15]

If the bread is made for commercial purposes it is permitted since it is not usually purchased in a social setting. The *Shulchan Aruch* allows this leniency only if Jewish bread is not available, whereas the *Rema* is lenient regarding commercial bread in all circumstances.[16]

(Note: this leniency obviously only applies if the bread is kosher and the only problem is that it was made by non-Jews).

In the Ten Days of Repentance between *Rosh haShanah* and *Yom Kippur* one should be extra cautious regarding *Pat Yisrael.*[17]

---

fall under the prohibition of *gevinat akum,* one should not publicize this ruling, since those who are lenient have opinions upon which they may rely. (*Iggerot Moshe* Y.D. 2/48).

13.   *Aruch haShulchan* Y.D. 115/16, *Chochmat Adam* 53/38.

14.   *Avodah Zarah* 35b, 36b. Despite the fact that the prohibition stems from the concern that eating the bread of non-Jews may ultimately lead to idol worship, *posekim* rule that even where this concern is not relevant, the prohibition still stands. Thus, for example, eating bread cooked by a Muslim is still prohibited despite the fact that Islam does not constitute idol worship. (*Peri Megadim Siftei Da'at* Y.D. 112/2).

15.   *Shulchan Aruch* Y.D. 112/9.

16.   *Shulchan Aruch* Y.D. 112/2.

17.   *Shulchan Aruch* O.C. 603/1.

COOKING BY NON-JEWS (בישול עכו"ם)

In addition to the prohibition of the bread of non-Jews the sages prohibited certain foods that were cooked by non-Jews. The reason for
this decree was twofold. Firstly, similar to *pat akum*, the sages wanted
to prevent intimate social interaction that could lead to intermarriage.[18]
Secondly, the sages were concerned that if a non-Jew prepared a meal
for a Jew, he might add something non-kosher to the food.[19]

In principle this prohibition applies even if the non-Jew is
employed by a Jew and there is less of a possibility of intimate social
interaction. Nevertheless some are lenient regarding this issue for people
who find themselves in difficult circumstances[20] and a rabbi should be
consulted for a ruling in such cases.

Which foods were included in the prohibition of *bishul akum*?
1. Foods served as a main course at a royal meal.
   The exact definition of this type of food changes according
   to place and time.
2. Foods that cannot be eaten raw.

There is no problem of *bishul akum* with fruits or jam etc.
Only a food which satisfies both conditions is prohibited.[21]

What level of Jewish participation is required in order to permit the food?
Sefaradim require a Jew to actually participate in the preparation of the
food in order for it to be permitted, such as by placing the food on the
fire, tempering the food etc.

Ashkenazim, as regarding *pat akum*, only require a Jew to turn on
the flame. In fact, it is even permitted for a non-Jew to transfer a flame

18. *Rashi Avodah Zara* 35b s.v. "vehashelakot", *Tosafot Avodah Zarah* 38a s.v. "ella".
19. *Rashi, Avodah Zara* 38a s.v. "miderabanan".
20. *Rema* Y.D. 113/4 with *Shach ad loc.* and *Chochmat Adam* 66/7.
21. *Shulchan Aruch* Y.D. 113/1.

lit by a Jew to light the oven.[22] Some even permit the food of a non-Jew if a Jew set a time-switch to commence the cooking process.[23]

In a case where a Sefaradi is a guest in a hotel or Jewish home where the Ashkenazi standards of *bishul akum* are met, there is basis for leniency which would permit him to eat the food.[24]

If *bishul akum* took place, the utensils should be cleaned thoroughly and may be used after being set aside for 24 hours.[25] The cooked food may not be eaten.

WINE OF NON-JEWS (סתם יין)

According to Torah law one may neither drink nor derive benefit from wine that was used for idol-worship. Wine of this type is known as *yayin nesech*.[26]

Later, the sages additionally prohibited drinking and deriving benefit from any wine of non-Jews even if it was not used for worship, in order to prevent social intimacy that could result in intermarriage.[27] Wine that is subject to this decree is known as *setam yeinam*.

Grape juice that was squeezed by a non-Jew before being boiled is also included in this prohibition.[28]

One may be lenient regarding deriving benefit from wine of non-Jews whose religion does not involve idol-worship (e.g., Muslims), as this is considered *setam yeinam*, yet the prohibition of drinking still stands.[29]

Even the wine of a Jew becomes forbidden if it is moved intentionally by a non-Jew in an open bottle or glass.[30]

If the non-Jew came into contact with a sealed bottle of wine, it does not become forbidden.[31]

---

22. *Shulchan Aruch* Y.D. 113/7.
23. *Minchat Yitzchak* 4/29.
24. *Yechaveh Da'at* 5/54, *Minchat Yitzchak* 7/2.
25. See *Kaf haChaim* Y.D. 113/90 and *Shach* ibid. 21.
26. *Avodah Zarah* 29b.
27. *Shabbat* 17b.
28. *Iggerot Moshe* Y.D. 1/50.
29. *Shulchan Aruch* Y.D. 124/6.
30. *Shulchan Aruch* Y.D. 123/1.
31. *Shulchan Aruch* Y.D. 130/1.

If a non-Jew came into contact with a bottle of wine belonging to a Jew after it had been cooked (*yayin mevushal*)[32] or pasteurized,[33] the wine does not become forbidden.

32. *Shulchan Aruch* Y.D. 123/3.
33. *Iggerot Moshe* Y.D. 3/31.

Glatt Kosher Meat
(בשר חלק)

In order for an animal to be permitted for consumption it must be slaughtered and checked for blemishes in accordance with the requirements of the *halacha*.

If before slaughtering, a blemish or incision is identified on the animal that renders it unable to survive, the animal is considered a *treifa* and may not be eaten even if slaughtered properly.[1]

However after the animal has been slaughtered and no blemishes are visible, we rely on the premise that most (kosher) animals are halachically fit for consumption (רוב בהמות כשרות).[2]

Nevertheless regarding blemishes that occur very frequently, we may not rely on the aforementioned premise and the animal must be checked even after slaughtering. One such blemish is an incision in the lung.[3]

1. *Chullin* 42a.
2. *Rashi Chullin* 12a. s.v. "Pesach".
3. *Shulchan Aruch* Y.D. 39/1.

47

After slaughtering, every animal has to have its lungs checked for an adhesion (*sircha*) which may be concealing an incision underneath it.

According to the *Shulchan Aruch*, once an adhesion has been detected the meat is forbidden.[4]

According to the *Rema* if an adhesion has been identified then it must be physically examined to determine whether it is detachable. If the *sircha* is detachable then the animal is kosher; if it is not then the animal is rendered *treif*.[5]

Sefaradi Jews follow the ruling of the *Shulchan Aruch* and do not eat any animal whose lungs were found with a *sircha* – hence the term "*glatt kosher*", "*glatt*" meaning "smooth" in Yiddish. (Or "חלק" in Hebrew).

Ashkenazi Jews follow the rulings of the *Rema* and permit eating animals found with a *sircha* on their lungs that has been checked. Nevertheless there are many Ashkenazim who follow the stringency of only eating *glatt kosher* meat.

There is room to be lenient for a Sefaradi who is a guest at an Ashekenazi's home where refusal to eat the food may cause embarrassment or animosity.[6] Similarly there may be room to be lenient for a Sefaradi who is in a situation where *glatt kosher* meat is not available, e.g., a soldier in the army.[7]

4. *Shulchan Aruch* Y.D. 39/10.
5. *Rema* Y.D. 39/13.
6. *Yabia Omer* Y.D. 5/3.
7. HaRav Mordechai Eliyahu זצ"ל.

Kashering Liver

Acording to Torah law, blood is forbidden to be eaten.[1] Consequently all meat today requires "salting" (*melicha*) after slaughtering in order to extract the blood.

Since liver is saturated with blood more than any other part of the animal's body, salting does not suffice and a more intensive *kashering* process is required[2] as follows:

1. If one is preparing a whole liver then one must cut it deeply along its length and breadth in order for the blood to exit when being roasted.

    If one is not roasting the liver whole but cutting it into two or three pieces, then one is not required to cut it as above.
2. It is customary to rinse the liver before roasting but if it was roasted without having previously being rinsed it is still kosher.
3. Ideally one should salt the liver before roasting. If the liver was not salted it is still kosher.

---

1. *Vayikra* 7/26.
2. *Shulchan Aruch* Y.D. 73/1.

4. The liver is roasted on an open flame on a grid that is designated only for *kashering* livers. The reason is that the grid may absorb blood from the liver during the roasting process and later release that forbidden taste into other foods.[3] Ideally the liver should be roasted until it is ready for consumption.[4]
5. It is customary to rinse the liver after it has been roasted.[5]

Note: One may *kasher* liver inside an oven, on condition that it is placed on a grid designated only for this purpose, and that an oven tray is placed beneath it in order to prevent the blood entering the oven itself.[6]

---

3. See *Shulchan Aruch* Y.D. 76/4.
4. *Taz* Y.D. 69/54.
5. *Rema* 73/1.
6. *Tzitz Eliezer* 11/53.

Kashrut of Eggs

When an egg has been fertilized, if it has blood in it, then the egg may not be eaten. This is because the blood comes from an embryo which would have otherwise grown into a bird and is therefore included in the prohibition of eating blood.[1] As such, fertilized eggs should be always checked for blood. If one forgot to do so, one may rely on the assumption that the egg has no blood in it, for most eggs do not. Similarly one may eat a hard boiled egg even though there is no possibility to check it.[2]

Blood found on unfertilized eggs is not forbidden. Nevertheless one should dispose of the blood since if consumed, people may come to think that one is eating blood that is forbidden (*mar'it ayin*).[3]

If one is not sure whether the egg with the blood-spot is fertilized or not, one may be lenient and use the egg after removing the blood, since most commercially produced eggs today are unfertilized.[4]

---

1. *Shulchan Aruch* Y.D. 66/2.
2. *Shulchan Aruch* Y.D. 66/8.
3. *Shulchan Aruch* Y.D. 66/7.
4. *Yabia Omer* Y.D. 3/2.

However, some opinions maintain that if it will not cause a financial loss one should be stringent and dispose of the entire egg, since there still remains a slight chance that it is fertilized.[5]

5.   *Iggerot Moshe* Y.D. 1/36.

Separation of Challa

There is a Torah commandment to separate a portion of dough before baking bread, and to give it to a *Kohen*.[1] The Torah obligation applies only in Israel and only when the majority of the Jewish population is residing there.[2] Therefore the obligation to separate *challa* today, both in Israel and in the Diaspora, is only Rabbinic.[3]

The obligation to separate *challa* only applies to dough made from "the five grains" i.e., wheat, rye, spelt, barley and oats.

The amount of *flour* which requires the separation of *challa* with a *beracha* is 1.666 kilograms.[4] Some *posekim* maintain that the measurement is 2.250 kilograms.[5] Nevertheless one should separate *challa* without a *beracha* if making dough from 1.200 kilograms[6].

Today there is no minimum amount of *challa* that must be

---

1. *Bamidbar* 15/17–21.
2. Rambam *Bikkurim* 5/5.
3. *Ibid Halacha* 7.
4. *Kuntres haShi'urim* (Rav Chaim Na'eh), *Yechaveh Da'at* 4/55.
5. *Shiurin deOrayta* according to the *Chazon Ish*.
6. *Kuntres haShi'urim*.

separated,[7] nevertheless the prevalent custom today is to separate a *ke'zayit* (15g).

If one is making dough in order to make pastries etc., one still has to separate *challa* with a *beracha* if it is going to be baked.

If one is making a thick dough which is going to be fried or cooked (e.g., spaghetti), one should separate without a *beracha*.[8]

One should try to refrain from making dough from flour and eggs only.[9]

After the separation, the *challa* has to be burnt (but not in an oven[10]) since we do not know who is a *Kohen* for certain.[11] There are *posekim* who hold that if burning is not a possibility, one may wrap up the *challa* in a double wrapping and throw it away.[12]

If one baked without separating *challa*, one should consult a Rabbi.

---

7. *Shulchan Aruch* Y.D. 322/1.
8. *Shach* Y.D. 329/4.
9. See *Shulchan Aruch* O.C. 462/5 with the *Mishna Berura ad loc.*
10. Since the *challa* is *issur*, baking it in a kosher oven will consequently render the oven *treif*.
11. *Shulchan Aruch* Y.D. 322/4.
12. *Minchat Yitzchak* 4/13.

Separation of Tithes[1]
(הפרשת תרומות ומעשרות)

A ccording to the *halacha* it is forbidden to eat or gain benefit from produce (grains, fruits, vegetables[2]) that were grown in Israel before separating tithes from them and giving them to the appropriate recipients (*Kohen, Levi,* and the needy).

Spices and tea leaves which are only used for taste are exempt from tithing, whilst those which are eaten need to be tithed.[3]

Note: In Israel today, even though most fresh produce is tithed, one should ensure that he buys his produce from a vendor with a reliable certificate of kashrut. The following laws apply to shops which do not carry a certificate, to a person's private produce, or to produce imported from Israel that does not carry reliable certification.

---

1. Special thanks to Rav Ezra Bick for reviewing this section.
2. On a Torah level the obligation to separate tithes is only on grains, grapes and oil (see *Bamidbar* 18/12).
3. *Derech Emunah – Terumot* 2/31.

Introductory concepts

Tevel: produce grown in Israel that has not yet been tithed.

Teruma Gedola: the first tithe to be taken from the produce.[4] This is given to the *Kohen*. *Teruma* has no specific measurement.[5] *Teruma* can only be eaten by verified *Kohanim* who are not in a state of defilement. Therefore today the *teruma* must be wrapped up and thrown away.

Ma'aser Rishon: a tenth of the produce. This must be given to the *Levi*.[6] Today we declare that a tenth belongs to the *Levi*. However since nobody can prove his *Levi* status one can eat the *ma'aser rishon* himself after "separating" it, since it is not forbidden to be consumed by non-*Levi'im*.

Terumat Ma'aser: a tenth of the *ma'aser rishon*. This is given to the *Kohen* by the *Levi*.[7] The same laws applying to *teruma* apply to *terumat ma'aser*.

Ma'aser Sheni: a tenth of the produce[8] separated in the first, second, fourth and fifth years of the seven year *shemita* cycle.[9]

In the Temple era, *ma'aser sheni* could only be eaten within the walls of Jerusalem. If the distance to Jerusalem was too far for the fruits to be carried there, the "holiness" of the produce could be transferred to a coin, thereby rendering the fruits permissible to eat as usual (*pidyon ma'aser sheni*). The money had to be taken to Jerusalem and used to purchase food to be eaten in Jerusalem, as is the law regarding *ma'aser sheni* itself.[10]

Today, one designates a coin for *pidyon ma'aser sheni* with which the produce is redeemed.

Ma'aser Ani: a tenth of the produce (remaining after separating

---

4. *Devarim* 18/4.
5. *Rambam Terumot* 3/1.
6. *Bamidbar* 18/24.
7. *Bamidbar* 18/26.
8. In essence this is a tenth of what is remaining of the fruits after separating *ma'aser rishon* i.e., 9% of the entire fruit.
9. The new year for vegetables is the first of *Tishrei* (*Rosh haShana*), whilst the new year for fruits is the fifteenth of *Shevat* (*Tu biShvat*).
10. *Devarim* 14/22–27.

ma'aser rishon), which is given to the poor in the third and sixth year of the *shemita* cycle.[11]

How to separate tithes

1. Each species of fruit must be tithed separately. For example, if one needed to tithe apples and oranges one would first tithe the apples and then the oranges.[12]

2. Take a little bit more than 1% of the fruits constituting *teruma gedola* and *terumat ma'aser*.

3. If one is in doubt as to whether tithes have been separated from the produce (this is known as *demai*), the text for separating tithes is recited with the omission of the *beracha*. However, if the produce being tithed has definitely not been tithed, the appropriate *beracha* is recited together with the text for separation of tithes found in an Israeli *siddur*. (This text also appears at the end of this section.)

4. The above amount should be wrapped up and thrown away.

5. (Today, *ma'aser rishon* is eaten by its original owner.)[13]

6. In years 1, 2, 4 and 5 of the *shemita* cycle, *ma'aser sheni* is "redeemed" onto a coin which is the local currency. The coin must be designated and set aside exclusively for this purpose.

7. The minimum value of this coin is a *peruta*[14]. If the coin is worth many *perutot* it can be used for redemption corresponding to the number of *perutot* the coin is worth. For example a coin containing 30 *perutot* can be used 30 times for redeeming *ma'aser sheni*. Once this coin is "filled", one can transfer its holiness onto a coin of smaller value which should be destroyed. Thus the bigger coin can once again be used for purposes of redemption.

8. If one is redeeming an amount of *ma'aser sheni* which is worth less than a *peruta*, it must be redeemed onto a coin which already

---

11. *Devarim* 14/28–29
12. *Mishna Terumot* 2/4.
13. *Chazon Ish – Shevi'it* 5/12.
14. A *peruta* is the value of 1/40 of a gram of silver.

contains a *peruta* of *ma'aser sheni* from a previous redeeming (*peruta chamura*).[15]

9. On *Erev Pesach* of the fourth and seventh year of the *shemita* cycle, the coins used previously for *ma'aser sheni* must be destroyed or cast in to the sea (*Bi'ur Ma'asrot*).[16]

10. In years 3 and 6 of the *shemita* cycle, *ma'aser ani* must be given to the poor. If this is impractical, one should loan to a charity organization the amount of *ma'aser* he assumes he will have to give in the coming year, and each time one declares *ma'aser* he should credit the organization as a partial payment of the loan.[17]

11. Fruits of the *shemita* year are exempt from *terumot* and *ma'asrot*.[18]

---

15. See *Bava Metzia* 52b.
16. *Yerushalmi Ma'aser Sheni* 5/3.
17. See *Mishna Ma'aser Sheni* 5/9.
18. *Rosh haShana* 15a, *Shulchan Aruch* Y.D. 331/19.

NUSACH OF SEPARATION OF TITHES[19]

In ארץ ישראל *on separating* תרומה *and* מעשר ראשון (*if there is doubt as to whether the* תרומה *and* מעשר ראשון *has been taken, the following blessing is not said, but the subsequent declaration is*):

בָּרוּךְ אַתָּה יהוה אֱלֹהֵינוּ מֶלֶךְ הָעוֹלָם, אֲשֶׁר קִדְּשָׁנוּ בְּמִצְוֹתָיו וְצִוָּנוּ לְהַפְרִישׁ תְּרוּמוֹת וּמַעַשְׂרוֹת.

מַה שֶּׁהוּא יוֹתֵר מֵאֶחָד מִמֵּאָה מִן הַכֹּל שֶׁיֵּשׁ כָּאן, הֲרֵי הוּא תְּרוּמָה גְדוֹלָה בִּצְפוֹנוֹ, וְהָאֶחָד מִמֵּאָה שֶׁנִּשְׁאַר כָּאן עִם תִּשְׁעָה חֲלָקִים כָּמוֹהוּ בַּצַּד הָעֶלְיוֹן שֶׁל הַפֵּרוֹת הַלָּלוּ, הֲרֵי הֵם מַעֲשֵׂר רִאשׁוֹן. אוֹתוֹ הָאֶחָד מִמֵּאָה שֶׁעֲשִׂיתִיו מַעֲשֵׂר רִאשׁוֹן הֲרֵי הוּא תְּרוּמַת מַעֲשֵׂר. עוֹד תִּשְׁעָה חֲלָקִים כָּאֵלֶּה בַּצַּד הַתַּחְתּוֹן שֶׁל הַפֵּרוֹת הֲרֵי הֵם מַעֲשֵׂר שֵׁנִי, וְאִם הֵם חַיָּבִים בְּמַעֲשַׂר עָנִי, הֲרֵי הֵם מַעֲשַׂר עָנִי.

In ארץ ישראל *on separating and redeeming the* מעשר שני (*if there is doubt as to whether the* מעשר שני *has been taken, the following blessing is not said, but the subsequent declaration is*):

בָּרוּךְ אַתָּה יהוה אֱלֹהֵינוּ מֶלֶךְ הָעוֹלָם, אֲשֶׁר קִדְּשָׁנוּ בְּמִצְוֹתָיו וְצִוָּנוּ עַל פִּדְיוֹן מַעֲשֵׂר שֵׁנִי.

מַעֲשֵׂר שֵׁנִי זֶה, הוּא וְחֻמְשׁוֹ, הֲרֵי הוּא מְחֻלָּל עַל פְּרוּטָה אַחַת מִן הַמַּטְבֵּעַ שֶׁיִּחַדְתִּי לְפִדְיוֹן מַעֲשֵׂר שֵׁנִי.

On taking חלה:

בָּרוּךְ אַתָּה יהוה אֱלֹהֵינוּ מֶלֶךְ הָעוֹלָם, אֲשֶׁר קִדְּשָׁנוּ בְּמִצְוֹתָיו וְצִוָּנוּ לְהַפְרִישׁ חַלָּה מִן הָעִסָּה.

On redeeming נטע רבעי:

בָּרוּךְ אַתָּה יהוה אֱלֹהֵינוּ מֶלֶךְ הָעוֹלָם, אֲשֶׁר קִדְּשָׁנוּ בְּמִצְוֹתָיו וְצִוָּנוּ עַל פִּדְיוֹן נֶטַע רְבָעִי.

19. Used with permission of Koren Publishers Jerusalem.

In Israel on separating teruma and first tithe (if there is doubt as to whether the teruma and first tithe has been taken, the following blessing is not said, but the subsequent declaration is):

Blessed are You, LORD our God, King of the Universe,
who has made us holy through His commandments,
and has commanded us to separate *terumot* and tithes.

Whatever [of the allocated portion] is more than one in a hundred of everything here, is hereby declared to be *teruma gedola* [the priestly portion] and is the northern portion. The one in a hundred that remains here, together with nine equal portions on the upper side of this produce are declared to be the first [levitical] tithe. The one in a hundred I have made first tithe is hereby declared to be *terumat maaser* [the tithe-of-the-tithe set aside for the priests]. Nine other equal portions on the lower side of the produce are declared to be second tithe, but if this produce must have the tithe of the poor separated from it, let them be the tithe of the poor.

In Israel on separating and redeeming the second tithe (if there is doubt as to whether the second tithe has been taken, the following blessing is not said, but the subsequent declaration is):

Blessed are You, LORD our God, King of the Universe,
who has made us holy through His commandments,
and has commanded us about the redemption of the second tithe.

This second tithe, together with its additional fifth, is hereby redeemed by one *peruta* of the coins I have set aside for the redemption of the second tithe.

On taking ḥalla:

Blessed are You, LORD our God, King of the Universe,
who has made us holy through His commandments,
and has commanded us to set aside ḥalla from the dough.

On redeeming fourth-year fruit:

Blessed are You, LORD our God, King of the Universe,
who has made us holy through His commandments,
and has commanded us about the redemption of fruit of the fourth year.

Glossary

Bassar be-Chalav (בשר בחלב) – Meat and milk: A (forbidden) mixture of meat and milk.

Bedi'eved (בדיעבד) – *Post factum*: An option considered halachically permissible but not preferred in the first instance (see *lechatchila*).

Bishul Akum (בישול עכו"ם) – *Cooking of non-Jews*: Any food cooked by non-Jews with insufficient Jewish participation.

Bittul (ביטול) – *Nullification*: When the taste of a forbidden food in a *ta'arovet* is nullified due to the preponderance of another food.

Bittul be-Shishim (ביטול בששים) – *Nullification in sixty*: When the quantity of the forbidden substance is less than a sixtieth of the mixture – the most common way of nullifying the taste of a forbidden food. See *bittul*.

Beriya (ברייה) – *A [complete] creature*: Certain substances are not subject to *bittul* if they are in the form in which they were originally created, referred to as *beriya*.

Chalav Akum (חלב עכו"ם) – *The milk of non-Jews*: Milk produced by a non-Jew with insufficient Jewish participation.

Chasalat (חסלט): Brand name of produce grown in insect-free greenhouses.

Davar Charif (דבר חריף) – *Sharp foods*: A food which tastes as strong as or stronger than a radish.

Glossary

Davar Gush (דבר גוש) – *A solid (cohesive) substance*: A solid substance which retains its heat after being cooked even when transferred to a new utensil.

Gevinat Akum (גבינת עכו״ם) – *Cheese of non-Jews*: Cheese prepared by a non-Jew with insufficient Jewish participation.

Hadacha (הדחה) – *Rinsing*: Rinsing one's mouth out to facilitate a transition, such as from milk to meat (under certain circumstances).

Hag'ala (הגעלה) – *Immersion in boiling water*: The process by which some utensils are made kosher through immersion in boiling water if they contain the taste of a non-kosher substance.

Hechsher (הכשר) – *A certification of suitability*: A certificate guaranteeing the kosher status of a food.

Heter (היתר) – *'Permitted'*: A permitted substance.

Issur (איסור) – *'Forbidden'*: A forbidden substance.

Kasher – *To make kosher*: To make utensils kosher for use.

Kavush (כבוש) – *Pickled*: According to Jewish law, a food that has been immersed in liquid for 24 hours (pickled) has the same status as cooked food.

Kedei Kelippa (כדי קליפה) – *The width of the shell, peel*: The outer layer of a foodstuff that has come into contact with a forbidden utensil or substance. Its thickness is defined as the minimally thick slice which one could cut off that would not disintegrate in the process.

Kedei Netilla (כדי נטילה) – *The width of taking*: The layer of food that has come into contact with a forbidden substance. Its thickness is defined as the width of a human thumb, or approximately 2 cm.

Keli Ben-Yomo (כלי בן יומו) – *A utensil used that day*: A utensil which has been used in the last twenty four hours and, as such, has food or taste particles absorbed into its walls which will affect the taste of any hot food that comes into contact with it.

Keli Rishon (כלי ראשון) – *Primary utensil*: This is the utensil in which the food was actually cooked (and it maintains this status even after being taken off the fire while it is still warm).

Keli she'eino Ben-Yomo (כלי שאינו בן יומו) – *A utensil not used that day*: If a utensil has not been used for twenty-four hours, the food particles in it are considered to be stale. The opposite of this is *keli ben-yomo*.

Keli Sheni (כלי שני) – *Secondary utensil*: The utensil into which the food is placed after it has been cooked. It is considered to cook less than the *keli rishon* as its walls are not initially hot.

Ke'vol'o kach poleto (כבולעו כך פולטו) – *As it is absorbed, so is it expelled*: The principle that one can make a utensil kosher using heat equal to (or greater than) that which caused the food or taste to be absorbed into it in the first place as the taste/prohibition is expunged in the same way that it is absorbed.

Kinu'ach (קינוח) – *Cleaning*: The requirement to eat something *pareve* which does not stick in one's mouth, under certain circumstances, to facilitate a transition, such as from milk to meat.

Lach (לח) – *Wet*: A liquid food.

Lach beLach (לח בלח) – *Moist with moist*: A *ta'arovet* of two liquid foods.

Lechatchila (לכתחילה) – *Ideally, At first*: The status or action considered most preferable by *halacha*; the recommended course of action in advance.

Libbun Kal (ליבון קל) – *A light burning*: Holding one side of a utensil over the fire until the other side, which is not over the fire, has become sufficiently hot so as to burn a straw or match.

Mikveh (מקוה) – *A pool of water*: A pool of water suitable for the immersion of people or utensils so as to purify them.

Mi'ut Matzuy (מיעוט מצוי) – *A significant minority*: A phenomenon which is in the minority, but common enough to cause halachic concern.

Nat bar Nat (נ"ט בר נ"ט) – *Secondary taste*: *Pareve* foods that were cooked in meat or milk utensils. See inside for the *halachot* governing this case.

Noten Ta'am Lifgam (נותן טעם לפגם) – *Gives a spoiled taste*: The taste given to food when cooked in a utensil not used previously for at least twenty four hours.

Peruta (פרוטה) – *A small coin*: The smallest denomination of currency used in Temple times; a coin of this value.

Pareve (פרווה) – *Neutral*: Food which contains neither the presence nor the taste of either milk or meat.

Pat Akum (פת עכו"ם) – *Bread of non-Jews*: Bread baked by a non-Jew with insufficient Jewish participation.

Posek (פוסק) – *Halalchic authority*: A rabbi who is considered to be sufficiently expert so as to serve as an authority on questions of *halacha* for the broader public.

Posekim (פוסקים) – *Halachic authorities*: Plural of *posek*.

Safek (ספק) – *Doubt*

Stam Yeinam (סתם יינם) – *Non-Jewish Wine*: Wine made by a non-Jew with insufficient Jewish participation.

Ta'am ke'Ikar (טעם כעיקר) – *The taste is like the essence*: The taste of food is considered to be akin to the actual substance. As such, if the taste of a food is present, *halacha* considers it as if the food itself were present.

Ta'arovet (תערובת) – *Mixture*: A combination that constitutes a halachic mixture.

Tevilat Kelim (טבילת כלים) – *Immersion of utensils*: The immersion of one's cooking and eating utensils in the waters of a *mikveh* as mandated by *halacha* if they were purchased from a non-Jew.

Treif – *Non-Kosher*: Food that is not kosher

Yad Soledet Bo (יד סולדת בו) – *One's hand recoils from it*: The level of heat at which taste is considered to be absorbed into a utensil and at which cooking is considered to occur. It is equivalent to 45°C (113°F).

Yavesh (יבש) – *Dry*: A solid food.

Yavesh beYavesh (יבש ביבש) – *Dry with dry*: A mixture (*ta'arovet*) of two solid foods.

Yein Nesech (יין נסך) – *Libated wine*: Wine prepared for the purposes of idol worship that is prohibited by Torah law.

Ze'ah (זיעה) – *Steam*: Steam released from food as it cooks.

About the Author

Rabbi Pinchas Cohen earned his *semikha* from the Israeli chief rabbinate and holds a degree in business management and psychology from the University of South Africa, as well as a B.Ed. from Herzog College. He currently teaches Gemara, *Hashkafa* and Halakha in the overseas program at Yeshivat Har Etzion.

koheinap@gmail.com

The fonts used in this book are from the Arno family